D0983995

Paul Revere

By Wil Mara

Consultant
Nanci R. Vargus, Ed.D.
Assistant Professor of Literacy
University of Indianapolis, Indianapolis, Indiana

Children's Press®
A Division of Scholastic Inc.
New York   Toronto   London   Auckland   Sydney
Mexico City   New Delhi   Hong Kong
Danbury, Connecticut

Designer: Herman Adler Design
Photo Researcher: Caroline Anderson
The photo on the cover shows Paul Revere.

Library of Congress Cataloging-in-Publication Data
Mara, Wil.
  Paul Revere / by Wil Mara.
    p. cm. – (Rookie biographies)
  Includes bibliographical references (p.   ) and index.
  ISBN 0-516-21841-7 (Lib. Bdg.)   0-516-25820-6 (Pbk.)
  1. Revere, Paul, 1735-1818–Juvenile literature. 2. Statesmen–Massachusetts–Biography–Juveni
literature. 3. Massachusetts—Biography–Juvenile literature. 4. Massachusetts–History–Revoluti
1775-1783–Juvenile literature. I. Title. II. Rookie biography.
  F69.R43M27 2004
  973.3'311'092–dc22

2004000429

In one night, Paul Revere helped change American history!

Revere was born in Boston, Massachusetts, in 1734.

He became a silversmith. A silversmith makes things like bowls and cups from silver.

Revere became famous for the things he made.

Revere became famous for another reason, too. He was an American patriot (PAY-tree-uht). That means he loved America.

At that time, the king of Great Britain ruled America. Patriots like Revere did not want a king. They wanted to be free.

9

John Hancock

The patriots had their own leaders. John Hancock was one of them.

Revere helped the leaders work against the king. He carried messages to leaders in different cities.

In 1773, Revere joined the Boston Tea Party. It was not really a party. A new tax on tea made the patriots angry.

So, they dressed as American Indians. Then, they threw boxes of tea from ships in Boston Harbor.

13

The Boston Tea Party made the king angry. He made new laws. These laws made more Americans want their freedom.

The king told one of his generals to stop the patriots from working against Great Britain.

The general sent his soldiers to catch the patriot leaders. The soldiers wore bright red coats. Patriots called them "redcoats."

18

The patriot leaders ran away from Boston. The general sent redcoats after them.

He also sent redcoats to find the guns the patriots were hiding. Revere had to warn the patriots.

On April 6, 1775, Revere crossed a river in a tiny boat. Then he borrowed a horse.

It was near midnight. As he rode, Revere yelled to wake people up.

Revere found the patriot leaders.
He told them the redcoats
were coming. The leaders got
away safely.

Then Revere rode to where the
patriots were hiding their guns.

The redcoats caught Revere, but they did not find the guns.

They met patriot soldiers instead. The fight for freedom began.

Revere served in the war.
It lasted eight years.

After the war, he started
a business. He used metal
to make things like bells.

Paul Revere died in 1818. In his life, Revere made many things. He also helped many people.

He will always be famous for his "Midnight Ride" to help Americans be free.

Words You Know

Boston Tea Party

John Hancock

king

"Midnight Ride"

redcoats

silversmith

Index

About the Author

More than fifty published books, including biographies, bear Wil Mara's name. He has written both fiction and nonfiction for both children and adults. He lives with his family in northern New Jersey.

Photo Credits

Photographs © 2004: Corbis Images: 14 (Bettmann), 17, 31 top right (Kelly-Mooney Photography); Hulton|Archive/Getty Images: 3, 13, 25, 30 top; Museum of Fine Arts, Boston, Gift of Joseph W. Revere, William B. Revere, and Edward H.R. Revere: 5, 31 bottom (30.781), cover (30.782); North Wind Picture Archives: 6, 10, 18, 30 bottom left; Stock Boston/Mike Mazzaschi: 29; Superstock, Inc.: 9, 30 bottom right (National Portrait Gallery, London, England), 21, 22, 31 top left; UnumProvident Corporation: 26 (artist, A. Lassell Ripley).

DATE		